UNINTERRUPTED

WORDS THAT COME OUT
FROM HEART.....

VANSHIKA MEHROTRA

ISBN 979-888530113-8

This is my first book which is going to be published , so I would like to dedicate this wonderful poetry book to my mom and dad.

Contents

Foreword

I am no such great expertise in writing poems or any literary works. These words have directly come out from my heart and I am obliged to share these feelings with the whole world. I hope every person who reads these poems will find peace and solace in their hearts.

1. MELTED WORDS

I always thought myself as flesh and bones
But you made me a human being !
I always thought myself as a machine
But you filled me with emotions !
I never knew what attachment meant
But realized it when it became hard for me to forget you !
I never knew what waiting for someone meant
Until I started missing you !
I never knew what caring meant
Until I started thinking about you !
The imperfect scars in me
Were filled by your perfect touch !

2. SILENCE WHICH CAN BE FELT

Never did I thought of being so close to you,
And will never be so close to anyone else.
Everyday I dream of us being together,
Cherishing the moments of our closeness ,
Hoping to relive those moments again !
Gathering strength from your memories ,
Gives me a reason to live everyday peacefully !

3. FAKE PROMISE

You promised to come back
Come back with a change ;
Perhaps I misunderstood the word 'change'...
You did come back
But only with your fake soul.
You asked me to wait
To wait for the right time ;
Alas I misunderstood the word 'right'...
You did wait for the right time
To move out from my life.
You asked me to recall our memories
If we ever move apart ;
I got confused this time
To recall , what?
The scars which you gave ,
Or , the love which you never gave ?

4. DARK AS HELL

Adorned with jewels,

Masked by powder on face ,

Wrists loaded with the bangles of burden ,

Ankles tied like a bird in a cage ,

Her head covered in a veil.

Unaware from the rest of the world

Her soul now confined in -

The four walls of her room

Dreams in her eyes,

Now lost like a mirage

In the desert.

5. CROSSED OUT

• 5 •

I want to fly
Fly away from all the shackles ,
Fly away from all my feelings ,
Fly up higher and higher ,
In the open sky , above all !
I want to run
Run away from all my thoughts ,
Run away from all my problems ,
Run away to find an escape
From this world !
I want to fight
Fight for myself ,
Fight with myself ,
In my life , alone from all !

6. MADE IT

To the one whom I thought
I would not be able to survive without ,
To the one wom I thought
As my life partner,
To the one whom I thought
Will be the forever love of my life ,
To the one whom I thought
Will forever stay in my heart ,
To that person I want to say that
I made it !
I survived the toughest days
Of my life ;
I found a partner
Within myself ;
I loved myself
A little more than you ;
I forever closed my heart
For people like you.
All these things
I made it
Without you !

7. CLOSURE OF MY HEART

I knew it was all over
When you fought with me
For someone else ;
Things now have changed ,
Priorities now are different ,
You moved on with a better one
I moved on for being my best .
I knew it was all over
When my heart stopped skipping for you
The same way it used to do before.
I knew it was all over
When you stopped understanding me
The way you used to do before.
I knew it was all over
The day I started getting scared
To share my problems with you.
I knew it was all over
When my heart decided to shut back
And not look back upon you
Any further !

www.ingramcontent.com/pod-product-compliance
Lightning Source LLC
Chambersburg PA
CBHW060951130726

48001CB00003B/1158